Praise for

Working Through the *Infinite* Source

"*Working Through the Infinite Source* is a reminder that one must be filled with faith and gratitude in order to make the journey through self-reflection and new thought. Through poetry, Sandeep guides you on this new path with the gentle reminder to always "have fun with it!"

– **Peggy McColl**, *New York Times* bestselling author

"Sandeep Agarwal has written a poetry book for anyone who is looking to set aside old paradigms and embark on a journey of self-discovery and living the highest version of oneself. Along with the beautiful illustrations of Valentina Fedorova, *Working Through the Infinite Source* is a must read!"

– **Judy O'Beirn**, CEO and President, Hasmark Publishing International

"From the beautiful and touching illustrations to the soul-stirring poetry and messages of love, hope, and gratitude, I enjoyed *everything* about this book! As a fellow poet and lifelong student of the infinite possibilities of the human spirit, I so appreciated the way Sandeep seamlessly blended these two things together to create such a magnificent collection of poems that will surely stand the test of time. If you've ever struggled to understand the meaning behind a poem, you will appreciate this author's thoughtful teachings and translations included at the end of each poem. Poetry is meant for everyone, and Sandeep does a beautiful job helping us bridge the gap so that we can truly find meaning and understanding in his beautiful words. I encourage you to read these poems over and over again, and allow the truth of their messages to touch your heart and soul."

– **Michele Marie Neyers**, International bestselling author of *3 Lines 30 Days—Unleash Your Inner Poet*

"Working with Sandeep has been a great journey. His creative yet strong style is visible in *Working Through the Infinite Source*, which reminds us of the beauty of our inner strength. Being his coach gives me immense pleasure, as he is an enlightened soul with a deep mission and purpose. Great poetry, deep messages, and attractive imagery make the book a must read."

– **Reetika Gupta Chaudhary**, Executive Coach, International Speaker, and Property Investor

"Mr. Sandeep shows strong passion and a high commitment to break free of old paradigms and alter his life as well as showing his dear love for his son! His poems always come with special vibration and inspiration through connecting with the Source, the unknown, the High Intelligence. As a life coach/mentor, I learn so much from his deep insights, especially the two fulcrums: faith and gratitude attitude! My life literally changes when I deepen these practices; confidence and liberation truly come. His dear love for his son is a fresh river running through this book, making this a must-read for children and teenagers to develop imagination, positivity, as well as a strong foundation for ultimate knowledge from the Source. I highly recommend the book for all kids, parents, and businesspeople who will love a fresh and positive stream from a highly knowledgeable poet."

– **Thuc Linh**, Life Coach/Co-Founder of Pure Coaching Vietnam

"Intensely expressive poetries. Sandeep has a special ability to get us to believe in ourselves. He has, through his poetic communication, captured the feelings of his own practice of credence in his highest ideals."

– **Premlata Agrawal**, 1st Indian woman to climb the seven summits, the seven highest continental peaks of the world including Mt Everest. Recipient of "Padma Shree" and "Tenzing Norgay National Adventure Award," among the highest civilian awards for excellence and adventure sports by the Government of India.

"We are one with the universe, all you've got to do is to become aware of this. It always looks after you and sends you the answers you need, the people and opportunities you've asked for and, sometimes, it also gives you a little "push" when you don't feel prepared. Sandeep's book will show you just that: that you are never alone and that the universe has your back."

– **Danielle Martins** , Branding Strategist and co-author of the bestselling book *Rising Up From Mental Slavery - How To Unleash Your Infinite Potential*

"To start with a very expressive cover page, you have beautifully captured emotions identified by each one of us. We only need to stop by and reflect on those. What makes your anthology unique is how effortless and uncomplicated it is in its words and yet, so deep in its intent. It is sure to make place in all age groups. The illustrations are alluring and artful. I couldn't help but go on to one after the other as you take us through a delightful journey of life's lessons! Indeed, life is a magical miracle and there is a child within us waiting to explore! Appreciate all your effort and looking forward to grabbing my copy soon!"

– **Punit Agarwal**, Serial Entrepreneur and Reading Enthusiast

"They say at the center of your being, you have all the answers; for a parent the child is the center of his universe, *Working Through the Infinite Source* takes you through that inner journey as an adult & beautifully expressed tales for your child! Mr. Sandeep, has described his imagination through heartwarming analogies & pictures – don't miss out reading them to your kids.
It's so hard to express in words how impactful it is!!"

– **Dishita Muliya**, Certified Life and Mindset coach & founder of Brain Secrets-Oman

"Sandeep's passion and artistic connection to Spirit allowed him to channel poems of wonder-filled universal truths. "Working Through the Infinite Source" is a true inspiration for the world and it has been a great honor to magically touch his *Welcoming The Paradigm Shift*. This is the path. Enjoy the journey!"

– **Nadine Bdil**, Award-Winning Growth & Success Mentor, InspireWorks.ch

Working through the Infinite Source

When we are connected to our Super-Being, all is possible!

SANDEEP M AGARWAL

Hasmark PUBLISHING INTERNATIONAL

Published by
Hasmark Publishing
www.hasmarkpublishing.com

First Edition

Cover Design and Book Layout: Anne Karklins
anne@hasmarkpublishing.com

Illustrator: Valentina Fedorova
vallllllintina@gmail.com

ISBN 13: 978-1-989756-85-0
ISBN 10: 1989756859

This book is dedicated with deep gratitude and love to our 'Maa and Bauji'. Though their physical presence was for a brief period in my life, their spiritual presence, with love and divine blessings, I can always feel each and every day!

Most humbly, to the galaxy of all the mentors, teachers, spiritual guides, coaches and people from all over the world they continually help me in my life and make it the most incredible journey. They stand like the lighthouse guiding my pathways.

To all my sisters, family members, friends, business associates and to my wife and son. Their love, support and good wishes have kept me moving swiftly in this journey.

And finally, with an incessant love to the ***Infinite Source*** *– the provider of all abundance and light, the source of all strength, the pure and formless one, the almighty, the all merciful... Present everywhere and within each soul!*

TABLE OF CONTENTS

Foreword	11
Preface	13
1. Working Through the Infinite Source	14
2. Universe is My Father	19
3. Lighthouse	22
4. Power of Gratitude	26
5. Why Are Goals Important?	30
6. Setting Objectives	34
7. Interviewing Yourself	38
8. Fake Fears	44
9. Calmness of Mind	48
10. Attitude Determines the Altitude	52
11. Pretty Much All Day Long	56
12. Life is a Magical Miracle	60
13. We Are the Light Bulb	64
14. We Have Two Selves	68
15. The Power of Autosuggestion	72
16. At the Halfway Mark	76

17. Seven Wonders of the Inner World 80

18. Have Fun with it! 84

19. If We Were So Simple 88

20. Rains and Rains Everywhere and the Child Within Us 92

21. Your Success is Absolutely Guaranteed 96

22. You Created History 100

23. Universe Beside on A Beautiful Long Ride 104

24. Say Yes to Dreams 108

25. Universe Wishes to Co-Create 112

26. Include Your Story 116

27. Invest in Yourself 120

28. The Creative Process (Divine Process) 126

29. Come Friends, Let's Go to the Beach 132

30. Welcoming the Paradigm Shift 136

About the Author 141

My Life and Journey 142

Why This Book? 144

When we are connected
to our Super-Being,
all is possible!

FOREWORD

I am so happy and deeply grateful that Sandeep has allowed me to write a few words for his remarkable book. This co-creation is a celestial dance. It is a dance of so many small vibrating particles that come from a Source of Love and Energy. It comes from deep within us and awakens our Souls to life by shining like sunrays.

I am profoundly touched by these beautiful poems that have awoken Sandeep's Soul. We are blessed that he is willing to share them with us. I have spent so much time speaking with Sandeep and know that you are in for a real awakening as his story is going to open your heart. It is an amazing gift to join him on a life-changing journey that brings messages of love, relationships, Shine of the Universe, Light in Darkness, Smiles and Faith; all offered by this most extraordinary, loving, spiritual person that I have ever met.

The message here is love, appreciation, and gratitude from son to father and father to son. Sandeep lost his father when he was 12. He misses him dearly still and the desire to give to his son all the support that he never had the chance to receive has fired up his heart.

This is yet another story, like mine, where the challenges of a pandemic, noticing personal paradigms and learning to change them, led to deciding to embark on the new journey towards light. Rather than getting stuck in the negativity of the current situation, Sandeep has created a key to new opportunities, and new friendships. Breaking free from the limiting beliefs and appreciating the side of Sandeep that desired success, peace, and abundance lead him to share his phenomenal story of the bond between father and son.

This book represents a focus on returning to the "source energy", the wisdom, the enlightenment, regaining power within you and re-connecting to a son that means the world to Sandeep. While I feel it is worthwhile to mention the old instances in a book, something that is beautiful, abundant, bright, bringing love and harmony in us. And references of past meeting new opportunities and dancing together balancing the energies and lifting the frequency of vibration only looking forward and upwards.

I love that Sandeep transformed his life and shows nothing but love, support, harmony, persistence, achievement, success, gift of giving and role modelling to his son, who adores him and looks up to him so much.
I celebrate the truth of awakening the children in bed, the ideas that were once dormant. I celebrate the rising of a desired state of consciousness. I celebrate the opening of our hearts, mind, and the senses which separate the seen from the unseen. I celebrate the co-creation as a celestial dance. I celebrate the unique and authentic story of Father and Son… And I welcome you to celebrate this magnificent story with me.

With all my love, from my heart to yours!

To my dearest friend Sandeep, who received my invisible power and light to guide him at his "sailing adventures".

Your "Lighthouse" and friend,
Vladimira Kuna
International bestselling Author of *The Bible of the Masterminds*

PREFACE

Working Through the Infinite Source I wish to tell that
I never deemed
An inner journey and a celestial show, was ever
thought and possible it seemed!

Through this book, the Infinite Source seems wish to reveal
That one is a medium and passage to its
unknown divine beam!

The poems are easy and lucid, and touch every realm
They have the power to take and to be at one's highest helm!

The book is not my personal journey
It is from the Universe to us, a revelation of
tremendous joyful learning!

That each one is capable of the Universal flow
Channelling is as easy and flashes by the source, as the
most enchanting welcome blow!

Come friends learn few tips, joyful to our every ribs
When poetry is easy, why ponder over lengthy prose?

When the Universe (The Infinite Source) is ready to work
with all its abundance and flow through us
Why then we seek the lesser resource?

Working
through
the
infinite
source
Best Seller

1. Working Through the Infinite Source

Working through the source, when one concept we learn
We assume, feel, and believe all work is done, before it is done!

The doer and doership is lost, what remains is the consciousness and the Infinite Source
To whatever name we assign God, Universe, Almighty or Energy divine!

Most magnificent works take shape
When one puts on this most graceful drape!

Through the blessings it is dawned
The simple and grateful heart when is born!

To this system when one starts to align
All fear sulk and great work starts happening to design!

One is in harmony and working with infinite store
The result unfolding and the doership no more!

Now when I recollect my mother's life
She followed this principle day and night!

To her blessings I now relate
This concept for me is new to operate!

Good readings and study helps us to revise
That working through the source will take the world by surprise!

The works which are done with happiness and spirit
They are the most rewarding and beautiful lyrics!

The work accomplished by working through the source
Enlivens the one and has a different force!

Great works have come through this 'Principle'
It is present wherever one sees and experiences excellence and exuberance!

It is the key to all Universal resource
When one works through the Infinite Source!

Working through the Infinite Source is when both the doer and the doership is lost, and one is perfectly aligned with the Universe. The Universe seemingly takes over all the actions and the most beautiful and magnificent work is rendered. One's work then becomes a beautiful lyric—a piece of art. Moreover, it renders the performer with feelings of joy and satisfaction. One must be filled with gratitude and simplicity to be eligible for this endeavour. The blessings and grace of one's parents, teachers, and mentors helps to dawn it faster. One begins to live and work in a flow and harmony with their infinite store house of abundance.

GLOSSARY

Line

2 assume, feel, and believe all work is done: creative process.

6 drape: attire, clothing.

7 dawned: becomes evident to the mind; be perceived or understood.

8 Simple and grateful heart when is born: one attains through simplicity and being grateful.

9 this system: life filled with gratitude and simplicity.

10 sulk: be silent out of disappointment.

23 Principle: fundamental truth.

24 exuberance: full of energy, cheerful.

25 Universal resource: all the magnificence, grandeur, and abundance Universe offers.

When we are connected
to our Super-Being,
all is possible!

2. Universe is My Father

Universe is my father
Just as the son holds his father's hands
So as I hold his strong arms!

He loves me all the while but sometimes scolds me too
So that I learn in his kingdom and achieve the highest expression of myself!

Sometimes he becomes the lighthouse guiding my ways on the rough seas
Whereas sometimes he is my guide showing me the 'unknown ways' to my pleas!

Sometimes he wears the garb of a mentor and reminds me to achieve success, peace, and glory
And tells me to break all my paradigms and limiting beliefs, attain my goals, and write a melodious story.

Sometimes he cracks a joke and laughs with me with his whole-hearted soul
Sometimes he celebrates and travels an extra mile and plays with me different roles!

Sometimes he sings the lullaby to help me to get to sleep
Sometimes he is the teacher who wakes me up from my ignorance and slumbering deep!

Sometimes he sits beside me and listens to my childish talking
And sometimes he makes me feel blissfully rocking!

The many roles he plays only a Father can do so
Sometimes he lifts me on his shoulders and sometimes holds my hand when we walk to and fro.

His arms are open for everyone and to every soul
The one who feels and trusts, the magic to them he unfolds!

As the great scriptures say "Our Father is in heaven"
But to my surprise and realization he is with us all day seven.

He is with us everywhere, in homes, offices, schools, factories, in all our cares and stories,
Helping us in all our endeavours, all our affairs, and all our glories.

I have found him becoming the captain, steering my ship on rough seas
He sends his guidance in the form of a lighthouse whenever a faithful heart needs!

He helps one cross the wild seas with zest and renewed vigour
Only one so keen can do so who is a fatherly figure!

Universal benevolence is present everywhere. A faithful heart acknowledges this fact and moves ahead in life. This poem depicts the parental love one feels when the Universe becomes one's fatherly figure. It also conveys that the Universe bestows divine guidance upon us at all times.

GLOSSARY

Line:

4 all the while: at all times.

4 but sometimes scolds me too: it seems that the Universe or nature have their own way of teaching the hard way through challenges and adverse situations, paving the way for one to learn and shine.

5 kingdom: world.

7 unknown ways: divine guidance; bringing in favourable people and situations.

8 garb of a mentor: arrives in the form of a teacher, mentor.

9 paradigms: habitual way of perceiving, doing, acting, and living. Paradigms are the programming and conditioning of the subconscious mind that controls the behaviour, thereby impacting the results in one's life.

14 childish talking: immature, silly, trifling, fanciful or juvenile talk.

17 lifts me on his shoulders: pampering.

19 magic to them he unfolds: he reveals the magic.

24 steering ship on rough seas: helping one through adversities and challenging times.

25 lighthouse: represents divine guidance provided by the Universe.

3. Lighthouse

Far out in the seas when the wild waves are raging and fierce
The ship trembles and shakes wildly with fears and tears!

The captain of the ship doing his best
But to all rescue now it seems to the nature it rest!

He is handling the ship with all his strive and praying to the lord for the light
So the seas are calm and he can arrive, leaving behind all the fright

When the coast is nowhere in sight
The violent waves toss fiercely the ship left and right
To that great rescue the prayers and blessings rest
The lighthouse by the heavenly Father is always sent

The ship sees new hope in this darkest night
The thunderstorms and rains falling with all their might
Far away a lighthouse is seen
Who brought it? Who was so keen?

To help one in the darkest night
When rains and waves thrust one's ship mercilessly aside
When one is not sure whether he will survive
To the coast and destination, he will finally arrive

At that very moment when the prayers and blessings meet
The lighthouse becomes ready to greet
Leading to the passage in this darkest night
To new vision bringing at sight and shining dazzling bright

The captain steers the ship using his forgotten skills
Now his focus has changed for the trip
His grip is tightened and rendered strong
The lighthouse can never go wrong
To numerous ships they have rescued before
They have always followed the great Father's accord

They are the master of this situation
They know the furious sea formation
They are abreast with such violent waves who in the stormy nights
Can overpower and drown the marvellous ships with all their might
They can put the best of the sailors to test
They can lead the ships to forever rest

The ship now in its heart it knows
The coast is near and so is the shore
It is now safe and in heavenly hands
With lighthouse guiding and is ready with sailor to all withstand

With new energy and delight
With faith in Universe and light
The ship is again cruising on wild seas
Now no fear is left, and enjoying the breeze
The heart is now calm, the lighthouse acts as the most
soothing balm

We are grateful to our Father on the ship
To send the lighthouse and tighten our grip
I can say for sure that our Father is not in heaven always
He is with us guiding in the stormy waves
He is very keen to all our slightest of pleas
With faith in heart and trust, he always brings the lighthouse
for rescue, on rough and raging seas!

Lighthouses have been the navigational guides and beacons of human civilization from time immemorial. They represent a source of guidance, illumination, steadfastness, protection, and salvation from harm and danger.

This poem signifies that when a person finds himself being trapped in the vagaries of life, both external and internal, one is in a state which is fearful, indecisive, and seemingly difficult to overcome. At that moment, when the earnest and faithful heart makes a plea to the Infinite Source, the Infinite Source sends the lighthouse signifying help from all directions and in various unexpected forms. With this divine support, the sailor along with the ship now finds new energy and inspiration and an illumined passage by which to cruise along the sea and finally arrive at the destination.

It reveals the very fact that the Universe is ever ready to help in all ways to the one with faith and a strong desire, embarking on a journey to alter his life. Lighthouses are always put in place by the heavenly Father to help, guide and lead the way with safety, joy, and pleasure.

GLOSSARY

Line:

1 Far out in the seas: far from land, coast.

1 wild waves are raging and fierce: suggestive of a very challenging situation; difficult to overcome.

2 ship trembles and shakes wildly with fears and tears: a person in a very fearful state, unable to think, almost losing hope.

22 dazzling bright: extremely bright light making one temporarily unable to see.

23 forgotten skills: suggesting a fearful state that makes one unable to use skills and take the right course of action.

28 accord: agreement.

30 furious sea formation: raging, angry, suggestive of extremely difficult times.

42 enjoying the breeze: signifies a relaxed mind and joyful state.

43 balm: fragrant cream or liquid used for healing.

45 tighten our grip: signifies our grip on our life.

47 stormy waves: internal and external challenges in one's life.

Gratitude

4. Power of Gratitude

So much has been said about gratitude
What magic does it hold?

To myself it kept amusing and thinking for long
Why is gratitude needed at all?

Then I realised through study, reflection, and experience that
words spoken with gratitude mellows down the listeners heart
But first it melts the one who says, before to others it finally
departs!

Mountains can be swayed with a feeling of gratefulness
One can tap into infinite universal resourcefulness!

In my life I have again and again noticed this truth divine
Whenever the world was too much for me, being grateful was
the most effective wine!

Storms passed by, the pandemics rolled
One with gratitude and faith was unscathed and standing tall

Never has this attitude, ever failed
When felt deeply and spoken with joy and faith, it has always
prevailed!

Being grateful is working with instruments of high precision
To nature it is the most favourite and highest possession!

In nature all is well and wisely put
The one with gratitude has the deepest root!

The most important is, it makes one sublime
One is open to every rhyme!

To him the seasons pass by happily and splendid
One who is thankful is most beautiful and remarkable indeed!

Try this attitude more often, it costs nothing as such
It is the 'no limit' credit card with the freedom to spend much!

The one spending is happy the most
The one receiving is joyfully enjoying the toast!

It is the world's best champagne
Just unbottle, drink, and cherish, and put a halt to all
inner rampage!

Gratitude is the language the angels understand
One who speaks and feels, he is in safer hands!

To this virtue when we imbibe
We melt the rocks with this inscribe!

It is the ordeal divine
When one is feeling low, he must follow this most
important sign!

Fill the life with gratitude
One will rise higher and higher reaching all altitudes!

Both in the inner and outer world
One will attain peace and joy without being whirled!

Let one plant the seeds of gratitude and wait
The one with a grateful heart always reaches the highest state!

Being grateful, thankful or having gratitude is the highest virtue a human being can possess. When one attaches the reason for why he is being grateful for a thing, person or situation one feels it more deeply. The magic of gratitude happens to the degree of one's feeling. One can be grateful to countless of things in everyday life, the list seems endless. The more grateful one feels the faster the life changes for good. The more one counts the blessings and be grateful, the more he sees magical changes in his life all around.

GLOSSARY

Line:

3 amusing and thinking for long: reasoning happily, thoughts entertaining in a cheerful way.

5 study, reflection and experience: process of understanding, assimilating and applying.

7 mountains can be swayed: mountains can be moved or cause to move.

8 tap into infinite universal resourcefulness: to establish connection with universal abundance, to use.

10 most effective wine: most effective remedy giving joyful solution, pleasurable.

12 unscathed: without suffering, unharmed.

30 safer hands: living under universal benevolence.

38 whirled: going round and round.

5. Why Are Goals Important?

Goals are the purpose in life
To which by a person abides!

To them who have; framed their goals
Blessings to them the life unfolds!

Goals give direction to living
Without them life is not becoming!

People with purpose have different approach
To them the world and ideas don't encroach!

Goals give command to the Universe and
creates a ripple
It conveys clearly the Demand Principle!

One who with a purpose lives
The Infinite Intelligence readily gives!

No goals are out of reach
Dropping the "how" the scriptures and mentors teach!

With faith and trust we gallantly march in a row
We cross all hurdles, like arrows shot from a bow

Goals should inspire and excite
Let us know the world our might!

To him no destination is afar
One who can conceive the goals, pursue
them with faith and believe, is soon
a star!

When we are connected
to our Super-Being,
all is possible!

Goals are the demands one lays out to oneself and the Universe. One sets the universal energy in motion for their fulfillment. It can be compared to making a call and the same is received by the receiver through the process of transmission and receiving. Unless the call is made, it can never be received. Goals set the creative process in action, whereby a person conceives, believes, becomes, and achieves. He who has goals in life, the external environment doesn't mean much as his focus is undivided. Like an arrow, one surpasses all resistance and hurdles very swiftly to finally hit the target.

GLOSSARY

Line:

1 purpose: the reason for existence, creation.

2 abides: accept or act in accordance with a decision.

4 life unfolds: providence giving away.

8 world and ideas don't encroach: overpower a person with ideas and thoughts. "World" here suggests external influences, while "ideas" suggest internal influences.

10 Demand Principle: demanding and believing that the goal is already achieved. Conceiving, believing,becoming and achieving (the creative process). Getting in harmony with your purpose and feeling and believing with faith that it has already been accomplished.

12 Infinite Intelligence: Universe, providence, infinite energy.

14 dropping the "how": leaving aside paradigms and limiting beliefs; pursuing goals with the feeling that the goal has already been achieved.

15 march in a row: working in alignment with oneself.

6. Setting Objectives

Setting objective is vital and important
It is essential for any accomplishment!

Setting them for achieving any task
Is the best thing one can do to start!

Make a list an evening before
For the work to be done the next day for sure!

Organising them in an array
Guide the way and make most of the day!

Progress can be measured and ascertained
When they are well defined and written!

They are the tools to the targets, goals, or purpose one wishes to accomplish
Setting them in advance lay the foundation for a good finish!

One waste too much time on "How"
Rather setting a goal and objectives to achieve and feel "Wow"!

Setting them lay a strong foundation
To the splendid outcome and structured advancement!

One brings a great value to him and the world
Who is conscious of them and lay unfurled!

Having them well written and in clear notation
Sets the universal energy in motion and rotation!

Nature has clear and well-defined objective
To have abundance for all and not selective!

If we can dwell on nature's call
Our dreams and visions we can make very tall!

One without objectives and goals strays in different direction
It's like a ship without a captain!

Small efforts and objectives each day
Can great oceans and mountains make way!

Once when a core goal is set, setting objectives is the next step towards fostering a clear understanding of the way to reach the desired outcome. The main difference between objectives and goals is that objectives are precise actions or measurable steps taken to move closer to the goal, whereas the goal or goals are the final outcome. Objectives are specific targets that typically have a time-bound schedule or timeline for completion for a structured advancement to the final outcome.

Objectives can be broken up into small time frames from yearly to monthly or even a daily basis helping to measure everyday progress. They help the person to channel his energy and focus and not let it dissipate into unproductive channels. With objectives and goals in place, the progress is phenomenal. They are the foundation for a good and successful finish.

GLOSSARY

Line:

1 objective: objectives are specific actions one takes within a certain timeframe to achieve goals. Goals are the final outcome; objectives help to achieve goals.

7 array: an ordered series or arrangement; displaying or arranging things in a particular way.

16 Structured advancement: moving forward, advancing, constructing, and putting together a plan in an organized, deliberate way.

18 unfurled: spread out, lay unfolded.

19 notation: a series or system of written symbols used to represent numbers, amounts, or elements in mathematics and music.

20 rotation: circular movement on its axis completing one full circle.

7. Interviewing Yourself

Did you ever imagine interviewing yourself?
The journey in the new realm!

One is the outer self, and the inner self being the soul divine.
This interview is unique and sublime!

Your inner self has been waiting for this one-to-one talk
It has been waiting to go along with you on a long walk!

Let's start and commence this most interesting journey
Begin the interview being uncanny!

"How are you sir?" the outer self asked
Starting the interview was the toughest task!

We have never interviewed our own self in pairs
To what it wants we have hardly ever cared!

We have given more importance to the opinion of others
It seems to one's inner self one has not conversed with for years!

The inner self replied "I am well and doing great these days"
"I am happy that finally you have laid the seeds and let in the rays!"

The rays of happiness and sunshine
Finally touching my core and my soul divine.

I was longing for this, for so long
Thank you, now that you have realised the song which was long forgone!

The outer self couldn't understand
It requested the inner self to further clear its stand!

The inner self spoke with more vigour and zest
It said, "Thank you again! for this new quest!"

The Inner self replied "I am welcoming the interview for putting me to test
Unless I take you to the highest creation, I will not rest"

Let us give this noble chance to our inner self to say its story
For once to take us back to the forgotten glory

The inner self said in a whispering voice "I am your best friend and your long-lasting love"
Let us stretch, flap our wings and fly higher like the beautiful white doves!

The outer self, surprised by this new encounter
The one he was searching for ages was so near and always present just across the counter!

He found the inner self to be most enchanting and attractive
The most beautiful and most cooperative

Something he never much cared, was his companion divine
Like refreshing and energetic Chardonnay wine!

The inner self spoke and spoke, sometimes loud and sometimes slow
The outer self listened and listened to this great flow, never ever he cherished a better speech in a row!

The interview finally came to a conclusive end
Both thanking each other as they stand

They embraced each other like very close friends
But in their hearts, they vowed to live this new trend.

They both knew they struck the deal
Which was a win-win for both, and an enormous steal!

Next day the story was published all over
Lovingly they stared at each other, relaxed and grateful for their glorious makeover!

We are so accustomed to the outer voices that we seldom notice the inner voice arising from our inner self. The above is one such journey where both the outer and inner self sit together for an interview with each other. The outer self is much surprised as the interview turns out to be the most exciting and amazing experience it has ever known.

One of the toughest interviews one can do is seemingly to interview one's own self. But if one can do this, it will turn out to be the most worthwhile experience, and one will arrive with surprisingly phenomenal results. One usually misses out on the most important and beautiful companion one has in the form of their inner self. Always guiding and helping in all our endeavours, it is ready to take us to the highest expression of our outer self. Only with perfect alignment with our inner self we can accomplish this feat. The poem also politely assigns the task to the reader to interview one's own self and suggests to not miss out on this great opportunity to meet and discuss with the most remarkable "Inner you."

GLOSSARY

Line:

2 realm: a field or domain of activity or interest.

4 sublime: of great excellence or beauty, unparalleled.

8 uncanny: strange or mysterious.

11 in pairs: in groups of two.

16 let in the rays: letting in sunshine, welcoming light.

23 zest: great enthusiasm and energy.

30 white doves: signifying new beginnings, peace, love, and prosperity.

*When we are connected
to our Super-Being,
all is possible!*

36 Chardonnay: A green-skinned grape variety used in the production of the world's most famous cherished white wine. The variety originated in the Burgundy wine region of eastern France but is now grown wherever wine is produced. Most notable regions are France, USA, Italy, Australia, New Zealand, Spain, Chile, Argentina, and South Africa.

43 struck the deal: come to an agreement.

44 enormous steal: having received by paying only a portion of the things real worth; an extremely good bargain.

46 makeover: a complete transformation of the appearance of someone or something.

8. Fake Fears

Fake fears are the fears manufactured by oneself
Just as one makes them, one needs them to destroy and tear!

Fake fears are false fears one creates out of thin air
With no substance, and nothing to care!

They are the ones which succumb great men away from glory
They need to be examined, tackled, and thrown away without a letter or story!

They drain brave men from vitality and fun
They train them for living a life merely of existence and without sun!

The trick to tackle them one must learn
One who made them must grapple them strongly at every turn!

Don't walk with them for long and make a close call
They have the knack to take a long stroll!

One who resolves in his mind to alter his life
No fear can exist in this clime and survive!

In one's heart, mind, and belief they seem to reside
Not for a moment must one take their side!

If one gives them energy and feed
They are sure to grab one's attention and read!

Throw them to the winds and cut them asunder
To the glory once more acquire and to greatness surrender!

They are the parasites which feeds day and night
In one's holy garden they tend to reside

Seeketh the help of the Universe, the supreme source
To beat them without any remorse!

Achieve thy infinite potential in store
Fake fears existence remaining no more!

Abundance and prosperity are our real nature
There is no place for false fears in one's stature!

Don't walk in their streets where they seem to reside
They appear to be sparkling bright and have tremendous might!

With faith, persistence, and wisdom
They can be thrown away from the great kingdom!

Know that we are the children of God Almighty
Fake fears now disturbing not slightly!

We are the sons and daughters of our 'Father in Heaven'
Why does then? From petty and trivial thoughts one has to struggle all day seven!

To fearlessness and freedom, we soar
Our pristine glory to the hearts we pour and restore!

Fake fears are the false fears we tend to carry that have no real substance and are fabricated by our minds. They drain human beings of vitality and fun and lead us to live a life filled with concern, anxiety, and agitation. Through learning, study and applying wisdom one understands the higher values of life; one by one these fears fall apart automatically. One's real nature is abundant, prosperous, and glorious. The practical tip of nipping such fears in the bud is extremely important as such fabricated fears show great might and strength if uncontrolled early. One should avoid giving them energy and nourishment and make an earnest effort to plant positive and creative thoughts leading to fearless and joyful living.

GLOSSARY

Line:

1 fake fears: thoughts creating an unpleasant emotion of being threatened, in danger or harm without any substance, fabricated, false fears.

1 manufactured: fabricated. Implies no existence in the first place, having been produced.

6 without a letter or story: without any importance, not supported by words or any justification.

8 Life merely of existence and without sun: living without any purpose, seemingly surrounded by darkness.

12 take a long stroll: accompany for a long leisurely walk.

14 clime: refers to climate.

19 cut them asunder: cut them apart.

20 greatness surrender: opening oneself to greatness, choosing greatness.

22 holy garden: the human mind is compared to a holy garden. Whatever one plants, one receives similar results.

24 without any remorse: without regret.

32 great kingdom: externally refers to the world, internally refers to the mind

34 disturbing: causing anxiety, agitating, perturbing.

38 pristine glory: original condition, unspoilt; implies the feeling of calmness and joy, which is our real nature.

9. Calmness of Mind

Calmness of mind is the secret to every endeavour
Its function is very similar to a fulcrum in a lever!

Achieving calmness is the greatest blessing
It is to all wounds, the most worthy dressing!

One who achieves calmness through understanding of the creative process
One is rightly on the path towards achieving success!

Yoga, deep breathing, exercise, and meditation are all wisely said
One can attain calmness through these well proven aids

Sometimes a journey to nature, meadows, mountains, and oceans we need
Sometimes only a deep thought can help to succeed!

When the mind is calm there is music in the air
Why not? To calmness we should always pair!

Calmness is derived from deep understanding
That we are full and without any void or lacking
The world and situations have the slightest impact
When we reconcile our thoughts and actions and make a harmonious pact.

When we realise and start feeling that abundance is our birth right
Believing that the Universe is always guiding us with its full might
No wonder one drives away all internal plight
Calmness is now easy with this new insight!

Quietness, relaxation, serenity, peace, and tranquillity are synonyms
Anxious, disturbance, agitation, restlessness, and distress are antonyms!

Let us leave the whole bunch of antonyms, discard and disregard
And just focus on synonyms, embrace, honour and accept the reward!

To one who can achieve all and shine
The only requisite is a calm mind!

Greatness and glory are always ready at one's disposal
One who with a calm mind can accept the divine proposal

When one starts relating to the higher laws and scheme
The thoughts get calmer and more serene!

Being calm and joyful is our natural state
One is blessed if to this simple truth one can relate.

Being calm and joyful is our natural state. One feels the lack or void though there is abundance all around in nature. When one turns his attention from the feeling of emptiness and gains insight to that of abundance and nature's bounty, the mind begins to become relatively calmer. The feeling of gratitude and gratefulness to nature, people, things, including ourselves at all levels further helps to reinstate and render the one practicing and feeling it to be more peaceful.

One's attention and focus must be constantly working on these principles at all times. Understanding the creative process is the key. Healthy living, yoga, meditation, wholesome food, and regular exercise plays a pivotal role in helping the mind and body to work in harmony. One with a calm mind is more creative and productive and thereby achieves success, prosperity, and progress in every aspect of life.

GLOSSARY

Line:

2 fulcrum: a pivot point around which a lever turns; something that plays a central role or is in the centre of a situation or activity.

5 creative process: working with the belief that it is already done; process of conceiving, believing, becoming, and achieving.

12 always pair: in harmony, working together.

14 void: empty.

19 internal plight: internal conflict, difficult situations.

20 insight: having a deep understanding or awareness.

28 divine proposal: divine, universal laws.

ALTITUDE
ATTITUDE
DETERMINES

10. Attitude Determines the Altitude

Hurdles and limitations are set aside
When one frames the right attitude in life!

All things seem possible to one
Whose attitude is in the perfect position!

Attitude is the "way one thinks, acts, and feels about anything"
It is the way one sees and relates to a situation, people, the world, and the things!

Situations being the same, the feelings are different
One with the right attitude can create beautiful summation!

To one the situation is always grim
Whose feelings for it have made them dim!

To one the situations are always right
Whose feelings have made them bright!

Mindset and attitude play a key role
They make the Universe answer one's clarion call!

Success is at one's doorstep and lap, it seems
When one develops positive attitude and takes a road map with dreams!

Often, we come in our ways
The limiting beliefs, wrong attitudes, and mindset usually take the goals away!

The goals which are near can seem so afar
With the wrong attitude fear grips too far!

Infuse the "gratitude" to set a right attitude calling
It is the most effective spanner to fixup and set right the
feelings and let them get rolling!

How high one moves in life and makes a killing
Is purely based on the right attitude instilling!

Approach life with playful spirit, gratitude and thanksgiving
The providence moves with a person with the right attitude
and believing!

One with right attitude, leaves sooner the past
To greater altitudes, the person moves up swiftly and very fast!

Having the right attitude is key for one's success. One can make or break a situation with a right or wrong attitude. One can develop and work upon setting them right through study and understanding. The study and observation of the exemplary lives of other successful people can also render one to develop them correctly. One can gradually instil the right attitudes and scale up to newer and higher altitudes.

Feelings of being able to serve or being of service, the spirit of being grateful, and thankful to others and nature is the key, and is a very effective method for developing the right attitude. When one embarks on this internal overhauling with earnestness and faith, no sooner one will be successful at all levels.

GLOSSARY

Line:

2 attitude: a way of feeling or acting towards a person, thing, or situation. Being passionate, dislike or like for a certain person or situation, and negativity or positivity towards life in general are all examples of an attitude.

4 perfect position: in the right position to help oneself.

8 summation: process of adding things together, summing up.

14 clarion call: a strong request for something to happen, a very clear message or instruction for action needed.

23 makes a killing: have great financial success.

AS A MAN
THINKETH

11. Pretty Much All Day Long

Pretty much all day long what one thinks, matters most
What one gives energy and thoughts, to that one's life toast!

If the thoughts rest on challenges and problems
The same arrives in abundance!

If the thoughts rest on opportunities and achievements
The same arrives and becomes one's life statement!

Hence think good and think positive
It takes a little effort, but it is essential and the only
effective method!

To one's life one moulds
Step by step unfolds!

The holy scriptures have discovered this truth long ago
As a man thinketh, so he becomes in a row!

One is rewarded day and night
If he thinks and acts right!

Life's abundance is open to one and all
One who thinks rightly wins the most
One who thinks wrongly loses the coast!

As men of learning have written long ago:

"The thought is a tool, which shapes are wills,
Bringing forth a million joys, and a million ills,
One thinks in his mind and it comes to a pass
The world is but a reflective glass".

Pretty much all day long one must replenish the thoughts,

With thoughts of abundance and prosperity
One shapes his life with boundless joy and clarity!

Friends, this simple truth of right thinking and living, when one learns
Life's bounty one enormously earns!

The poem brings home the point of the difference that the right thoughts and actions can play in one's life: they can make or break us. From time immemorial every scripture and teachings have reconciled to this very fact that "As a man thinketh so shall he become." Hence one needs to be watchful of their thoughts and actions at all times for a joyful, peaceful, and abundant living.

GLOSSARY

Line:

2 gives energy: giving focus and attention, being associated.

2 one's life toast: honouring the experiences that define who we are and where we're headed.

6 life statement: memoir, life story.

12 becomes in a row: becomes in succession.

17 loses the coast: loses the objective

21 comes to a pass: happens, occurs.

22 reflective glass: acting as a mirror.

12. Life is A Magical Miracle

Life is a magical miracle
Defying all logic and shackles!

When "logic" and "how" are sometimes kept at bay
Life is a path full of miracles and magical arrays!

The merging of the conscious and subconscious mind is a celestial marriage
Joy, glory, and peace are its carriage!

Gratitude, faith, love, and earnestness are the fulcrum and the substratum
Where every thought and beings thrives, achieves success, glory and finds equilibrium!

A human mind working with gratitude, faith, love, and earnestness finds a perfect calm and balance. One's actions then leads him to success and glory. Trusting in the higher purpose, one loses the tendency to focus too much on how and logic. The mind is not working in conflict, but rather is working in perfect harmony to accomplish the aim and definite goals. The whole energy is working in tandem and not dissipated through various unproductive channels. The result is joy, glory, and peace—life becomes full of magic and miracles!

When we are connected
to our Super-Being,
all is possible!

GLOSSARY

Line:

4 arrays: an impressive display, or an arrangement displayed in a particular way.

5 The merging of the conscious and subconscious is a celestial marriage: when both the conscious and subconscious minds are working together in harmony, a higher state of being in perfect alignment.

7 life statement: memoir, life story. fulcrum and the substratum: foundational; playing a central or essential role in an activity, event, or situation.

8 finds equilibrium: finds a calm state of mind; a perfect balance.

13. We Are the Light Bulb

We are the light bulb
We need to illumine ourselves before illuminating others!

We are the flowers
Which need to blossom first before becoming a sight of joy to many!

We are the fragrance
Which needs to be drawn out from the flowers initially and undergo a process before it can be turned into the fragrant perfume!

We are the magnets
Which need to gain its properties of attraction before being able to attract goodness and joy!

We are that who first needs to understand "who am I?"
Thereafter we can communicate to others effectively "who they are"!

Life is first becoming and later imparting to someone else
Becoming first the cradle of joy before giving!

The poem brings home the important message that one must enlighten himself before he can truly be capable of enlightening others. Unless one is a source of anything, he cannot give it to others. One first needs to undergo the process and attain clarity and understanding for a effective and beneficial communication. The poem tries to say that one can effectively communicate to the extent that one has unfolded one's own self.

When we are connected
to our Super-Being,
all is possible!

GLOSSARY

Line:

2 illumine: to gain knowledge, fill with light, enlighten.

4 to blossom: state of bearing flowers.

6 turned into the fragrant perfume: the process by which fragrance from flowers is turned into perfume denotes how one undergoes learning and implementation of the learning before being able to communicate to the world.

8 gain its properties of attraction: ingrain learning; to acquire; reference to a magnet implies the process of magnetism through which a metal turns into a magnet.

9 understand "who am I?": with respect to knowing oneself spiritually; to assess oneself.

10 communicate to others: communicating/assessing others after knowing oneself; one must first enlighten himself before enlightening others.

12 cradle of joy: source, origin of joy

14. We Have Two Selves

We have two selves

One is relatively bold and unfolding new dimensions
One is entirely cold and holding old paradigms!

One is objective and seeing abundance and prosperity
One is subjective and seeing limiting beliefs and disparity!

One is thriving, believing, desiring of success, victory, and treat
While the other is just surviving, believing and wanting to recess, retreat, and defeat!

One is going "all out" for expression and accomplishing definite goals
One is going "all in" for suppression and lack of any roles!

As the man of learning says: the one which we feed and fuel, will grow
The other one without the right feed and fuel will definitely be slow!

As nature reveals, the one which you give water and manure will survive
Whether it is weeds or flowers, it's on us to support and see which one to thrive!
Though weeds have tendency to grow by themselves and take-over the garden being stubborn and stout
Unless the gardener is alert and makes a conscious effort to drive them all out!

Let us take care of the objective, dreaming, achieving, and believing self
Nourish it with our love, support, honour, appreciation, and care!

The two selves are the two sides of the same coin
Nature has given the choice to us to decide whether to thrive or just survive
It all depends entirely on us which self
to revive and which self to deprive!

Let us follow the Inner wisdom
and guidance
Which helps the beings
make the right choice
and prudent decision!

When we are connected
to our Super-Being,
all is possible!

The poem suggests that human beings have two facets in their personality: One welcomes the change and is ready to accept knowledge and alter their life for a bigger, bolder scheme; whereas there is one facet among their personality which holds on to the limiting beliefs and is averse to change. The human mind is like a garden and needs conscious effort to keep it beautiful. Whichever version he feeds will be the one to grow and thrive. It takes constant effort to uplift oneself. The mind, like fertile soil, flourishes whatever is sown into it.

GLOSSARY

Line:

2 unfolding new dimensions: open to new knowledge.

3 old paradigms: limiting beliefs, averse to change.

14 being stubborn and stout: one sees that there is a general tendency to fuel negativity; positive thoughts need constant efforts to work upon and be made part of one's life, whereas negative thoughts grow by themselves and need constant efforts to drive them out from our minds.

15 gardener: us, as the master of our own lives.

19 nature has given the choice: one has the choice to mould his life the way one wants.

I am a bestselling author
I am confident
I believe in my Self
Universe helping me

15. The Power of Autosuggestion

Autosuggestion is scripting our lives
With affirmations and positive vibes!

It is the tool for the earnest seeker to follow
They alter their lives steadily and slow!

They are a pep talk for oneself to trace
To think and align back to grace!

One chooses the life the way he wants
It is the most effective tool to get them all!

Feelings and right actions when mixed with this trickster
With them all well placed, you will hit the sixer!

The subconscious mind is ready to go
With words when filled with right feelings spoken to it in a flow!

To inner communication your results do matter
One is more productive without much outside chatter!

To make the desire a burning obsession
It needs the spark of positive autosuggestion!

Faith and persistence are its long-term friends
It's the most ancient as well as the newest of trends!

The fulfillment of our desires depends on services we can render
One must include this "principle of exchange" and remember!
One who is ready to serve
Is capable of touching every nerve!

The Universe will surely unfold
To oneself with absolute faith if one has told!

One is the master of his fate
If positive autosuggestions are one's roommate!

One is the captain of his soul
If strong beliefs and affirmations one has secretly to one's mind installed!

One has the power to influence his life with new thoughts arising from mind
If one is ready to unlearn and rewind!

Principles of success are laid widespread
One who impresses them inside can effectively tread!

Autosuggestion is the most important tool
It is to our mind the most efficient fuel!

One's mind is a rich and fertile garden
When one sows the thoughts of creative nature!

Positive suggestions are the music divine
When one feeds them to the mind, they have an effect sublime!

We are nature's most creative and imaginative tribe
It is essential to convey to oneself this time tested and proven scribe!

Autosuggestion and affirmations are powerful tools proven over the period of time for self-development. One can script and reprogram his life by autosuggesting himself with positive statements. They are not only music to our ears—but also to the mind and soul. One can steer one's life by effectively and rightly using them. Coupled with correct actions and feelings, they have the power to drive human beings and lead them to success and glory.

GLOSSARY

Line:

1 scripting our lives: the way we want our lives to be.

3 earnest seeker: one living with definite purpose.

5 pep talk: intended to arouse enthusiasm and increase determination to succeed.

9 trickster: in mythology, a trickster is a character in a story who exhibits a great degree of intellect or secret knowledge and uses it to play tricks, one who disobey normal rules and defy conventional behaviour. With reference to autosuggestion, they work as a trickster to magically alter one's life.

10 hit the sixer: hit for the maximum run in a cricket match; achieving maximum success and results.

12 spoken to it in a flow: spoken to one's own self rightly.

14 chatter: talks without much substance; idle words.

32 tread: walk in a specified way; leading life in a particular way.

39 imaginative tribe: imaginative community, group, or society.

40 proven scribe: proven words.

16. At the Halfway Mark

Once you decide to alter your life
You are already at the halfway mark in this great strive!

Kudos to you and congratulations
For making this extraordinary decision!

Remember all the great lessons
To remain positive and keep congratulating yourself in all sessions!

Feel really good about embarking on this journey
You are the chosen few by the great Attorney!

Life's lessons are always learnt
Sometimes easy, sometimes with sharp turns!

One with persistence and faith leads
To him the life is an easy streak!

Bubbling over with joy and delight
The other half is very near in sight!

Head on with the mentor's words
Clearing the skies like the swift birds!

The goals are near just one more flight
Flap your wings with all your might!

Sing songs of happiness and joy
Feeling that you have already arrived!

FINISH

The world will soon see your light
To our inner self we re-unite!

Long has one lived the life of doubts and indecision
Now be blown out with your shots in utter precision!

Life is waiting to embrace
Achieve abundance and eternal grace!

You are already at the halfway mark
Just be ready to disembark!

Usually, people have difficulty making decisions, particularly when it comes to altering their limiting beliefs and paradigms. But when one decides to do so, he is already at the halfway mark towards his destination or goal. Unless one decides, he is unable to move forward and take the required course of action. One's indecisiveness keeps one holding to old ways of living.

Life is waiting for us to flap our wings with all our might and fly higher and higher. Life is easy for one who keeps oneself open to new experiences. One unlocks the abundant potential that nature has to offer. One is ready for disembarkation shortly. The destination which seemed far away was much nearer.

GLOSSARY

Line:

2 great strive: make great efforts to achieve or obtain something; great struggle.

3 kudos: praise, accolades, credit for one's achievements.

6 keep congratulating yourself in all sessions: continue to inspire yourself.

8 great Attorney: the Almighty, the Universe.

12 easy streak: uninterrupted spell; series.

16 swift birds: highly aerial birds.

18 flap your wings: put in more effort.

21 your light: your energy, glory.

28 disembark: getting ready to arrive.

17. Seven Wonders of the Inner World

Time since when we were small
To our ears, "Seven Wonders of the World" has been constantly told!

But when I grew up wise
I realised that "Seven Wonders of the Inner World" stood
equally magnificent and bold!

Just as the seven wonders enchant humanity
The seven wonders of the inner world bring serenity
and prosperity!

To the readers much surprise
Let me one by one them apprise!

Imagination and creativity are the first wonders
Human beings possess
They make castles out of thin air
To the unknown realms they dare!

Faith and trust are the second wonders
One who possesseth one knows
One sings the songs like a morning bird
Before the day has still not dawned!

Persistence and consistency are the third wonders
The chosen one develops and cares
The goals set are accomplished and done
With still time to spare!

The fourth wonders are discipline and earnestness
The great mantra for success
One who instils them in his strive
Never falters in his life!

The fifth wonders are confidence and self-belief
Men of learning have conveyed again and again to our relief
One who follows them day and night and chimes
Makes the hay at all times!

The sixth being decision power
The origin of every goal and aim
When one decides with a firm resolve one's task
Even Providence dare not him to ask!

The seventh being desire and ambition
They are the foundation of every generation
One who lays them in sound formation
Sets the Universal energy in great motion

The outer wonders have sometimes conflict over each other
The inner wonders are always in spirit with one another

To such wondrous power we belong
The wonders of the inner world are playing a constant song

The wonders of outer world are all well and good
One has succeeded, if to the inner wonders one has aligned
and stood

They are waiting for our chores
They are ready to put any scores

The earnest student who possesses and ingrains
To him the Universe grants all gains

One who gives them due respect
Achieves success and creates a deep impact!

The outer world is beautiful with ancient and modern structures
The inner world is astounding with these timeless features!

Though they don't compete
Let us not only to outer wonders restrict and retreat
The inner wonders are our very essence
We are miracles and infinite with their very presence!

The poem depicts that in pursuit of outer things of joy one often forgets the inner joy which can be obtained through harnessing our own inner resources. One often misses the rare qualities one possesses to achieve success, peace, joy, and to live an abundant life. The inner qualities are not less than wonders which can take a person to the pinnacle of whatever he desires to accomplish in life. We are remarkable, and the epitome of creation with the very presence of these inner wonders.

GLOSSARY

Line:

2 constantly told: very often or repeatedly heard.

8 apprise: inform or tell someone.

20 still time to spare: accomplishing aims and goals well within the targeted time frame, or before.

32 providence dare not him to ask: Universe supporting completely.

36 great motion: set rolling in movement, provide impetus.

37 conflict over each other: disagreement between people to which one should be included or excluded. In reference to the poem, it means the conflict and disagreement between people all over the world as to which wonder should be part of the 'seven wonders of the world' list.

38 spirit with one another: working in harmony once the specific ideal is assigned; working together.

43 our chores: tedious but necessary tasks; implies to continue working on upgrading oneself through various means.

52 retreat: go for a short break to relax or travel.

18. Have Fun with it!

Have we ever realised that injecting fun in all activity
Is essential and vital and bursts creativity?

Without fun, life is dull and boring
To so many tasks we shall just be snoring!

The work gets better progressively
When it is instilled with fun successively!

Others feel our energy and the work reflects radiance
When it is drenched with fun, enjoyment, and exuberance!

The dictionary meaning of fun is:
Enjoyment, amusement or light-hearted pleasure,
It is mostly associated with children, as they it in abundance
do treasure!

Why can't we adults at times adopt
Children's ways to instil fun and take life as abundant
and prompt?

The nature for same reason hath gift do children gave
It created everything with fun and rave!

If we can understand the nature's creation
Every act is done with joy and recreation!

If we change the way we look at things with fun
We experience positive outcome!

Let us follow the nature's rage
Some fun we add to our daily page
Let us ingrain in our daily run, some joy, pleasure, and lots
of fun!

Sometimes it is his, sometimes it is her turn
Why not live our life with cheerfulness and learn!

When one is working with fun, one is in a great vibration
As the divine law works, one attracts favourable situations!

Working with enjoyment one is manifesting true potential
With a higher frequency and acceleration!

Our goals near and the path wonderful rendition
When we submit with fun to providence our petition!

Fun, though a word often associated with children, actually resonates deeply with all of humanity. Any activity done with fun renders the work exciting and full of energy. Beautiful work is the result when activities are done with fun and joy. If one sees all around, one realises that nature has created everything with joy and divine purpose, it seems it has created all with fun. Without injecting the fun, the tasks may often become boring and providing no impetus to the doer.

GLOSSARY

Line:

1 injecting: introducing something with force or pressure.

2 bursts creativity: sudden outbreak of creative ideas.

4 snoring: asleep.

6 successively: uninterrupted sequence.

8 exuberance: full of energy, excitement, and cheerfulness.

14 hath: have (old English).

15 rave: lively party or atmosphere with dancing and drinks.

20 rage: showing strong feelings, desire, passion, intensity.

23 sometimes it is his, sometimes it is her turn: covering entire spectrum of human beings; pairs of opposites.

27 manifesting: clear or obvious to the eye or mind.

29 rendition: performance, especially in relation to a drama or piece of music.

30 to providence our petition: a respectful and humble request to nature, spiritual power, God.

19. If We Were So Simple

To flutter and dance in the breeze as plants do.

To blossom and be ecstatic in the rains as flowers do.

If we were so simple …

To be like a new-born in an eternal peace and calm.

To be like kids playing in the rain in puddles and making sandcastles on the beach.

If we were so simple …

To be meditative and trusting the Universe for goals already accomplished.

To be in an orchestra and know that each one would play beautiful music.

If we were so simple …

To be as a rainbow with different colours; and a sight of beauty to many.

If we were so simple …

To be as rivers constantly flowing and nourishing the life, and knowing that their
final destination is merging with the infinite ocean.

If we were so simple …

To be as birds soaring high and realising the ability to fly; and being grateful knowing that flying higher is the gift being bestowed to them lovingly by the Father Almighty!

If we were so simple … to know that being simple is our original nature …

When we are connected
to our Super-Being,
all is possible!

Everything we see in nature is simple; it is what it is. When one realises nature's way, one starts living a natural life in harmony with himself and others. Life then unfolds its beautiful music, and the world becomes a grand orchestra. One understands that one is a part of this grand orchestra and is playing his part. It also suggests being grateful and having deep gratitude towards nature, and towards the Father Almighty for His benevolence and abundance.

GLOSSARY

Line:

2 be ecstatic: feeling or expressing overwhelming happiness or joyful excitement.

7 trusting the Universe: being confident of oneself; providence.

13 final destination: achieving one's highest potential; achieving goals.

13 merging with the infinite ocean: realising that we are infinite beings.

14 Father Almighty: Nature, Universe; the Source.

20. Rains and Rains Everywhere and the Child Within Us

It is raining cats and dogs,
Morning sun nowhere in sight!

It's pitch dark; and rains and rains everywhere with all their might!
The pouring down is so much,
The thunderous rains to the heart touch!

The morning birds wanting to take the flight,
Are unable to do so with nowhere in sight!

Lo! There is some distant bird chirping and attempting to take a flight
Life in a new way is resonating with all her light!

The heart is in blissful solitude,
Life is cherishing the new attitude and feelings of gratitude!

The rains have drenched the whole landscape and ground,
As children do, I wish to get wet and dance with joyful solace and splash water all around!

An early morning heavy downpour has drenched the whole view with water. Water is all around. One is feeling peace and joy. Nature has filled the earth with its bounty. There is abundance all around. One has dropped the old paradigms and limiting beliefs and has now acquired a new attitude. With gratitude in heart, he is enjoying nature's bounty (rains). He wishes to joyfully share his knowledge and learning with others.

When we are connected
to our Super-Being,
all is possible!

GLOSSARY

Line:

3 rains and rains everywhere with all their might: heavy downpour.

9 life in a new way is resonating with all her light: With darkness dispelling one expressing fully, living to his full potential.

10 the heart is in blissful solitude: extremely happy; having a peaceful and calm state of mind.

11 new attitude: breaking the old paradigms and beliefs; establishing new thought processes and a new mindset.

13 joyful solace: feeling of joy and peace.

13 splash water all around: to spread and scatter the joy and learnings all around with others.

21. Your Success is Absolutely Guaranteed

With aims and objectives in place, the right attitude, a calm mind and faith when one heeds
One's success is absolutely guaranteed!

Failure cannot touch a man
If he follows this wisdom clan!

Conceiving, believing, and becoming are the keys
One's success is absolutely guaranteed!

Weakness of attention and poverty of imagination have taken a long toll
Let the person on the path of success break them all!

One should root away one by one and become sublime
Alter the old belief system and paradigms!

One's beliefs have withheld and put one out of track
It is now time to awake, arise, think, act; and leave behind all setbacks!

Success is waiting at our doorstep
Let us welcome this new fest with all our zest!

Thoughts of failure grind and kill
Now they are thrown out to the wind!

Their ribs are shattered and tattered away
Fake fears take beings for a wild sway!

The Learned from their experience teach
One's thoughts and actions lead one to reach!

MY SUCCESS IS
GUARANTEED
100%

Tall mountains are not so difficult to scale
When one's heart is set on success tales!

Great work and progress are waiting to happen and rule
When we feel we are already successful!

When we connect outcomes each day with feelings and emotions
That is the key to set the Universe in motion!

Success and failure are two sides of the same coin
The one we feed wins, shines and chime
The other one loses its climb.

The seeds of success when are sown
The pastures are greener and well grown!

It takes just a short while and efforts to realise that our
'Success is absolutely guaranteed'
One needs to feel as if it is already done, to be in the most successful creed!

The poem suggests that one following the path of creative process is sure to attain success. When one operates with set objectives, the right attitude, a calm mind and faith, one's success is absolutely guaranteed. The heart and mind already believing in success drives the Universal energy in motion and helps the seeker finally accomplish his goals.

GLOSSARY

Line:

1 heed: pay attention, take notice.

4 clan: a group of people associated by a lineage, descended from a common ancestor.

5 Conceiving, believing, and becoming: creative process.

7 weakness of attention and poverty of imagination: mental limitations.

9 sublime: of great excellence, beauty.

10 paradigms: behavioural patterns.

22 success tales: tales of inspiration, success stories.

26 Universe in motion: Universe working with you to make things happen; divine guidance.

28 chime: to be in agreement with, melodious a ringing sound.

29 loses its climb: loses strength to move.

33 creed: a set of beliefs or aims which guide someone's actions.

22. You Created History

Just by sticking to your goals
Playing yourself in perfect roles!

You created history
You unravelled all the mystery!

With lighting speed, you are travelling
All desires accomplished, perfectly revelling!

You are floating over clouds with happiness and ease
The world is now a fabric without a crease!

When you are strong you are creative
One learns to live life without sedatives!

You are writing your own script
Filled with abundance and Joy!

The world is appreciating
Your narratives without any ploy!

All arts and skills one have learnt in fray
Now one knows for sure the Universal way!

One has learnt that giving and serving is the key
One cannot achieve without paying this fee!

You have created the history, it's your time in a row
Rejoice and enjoy and go with the flow!

Keep the momentum, the learning should go on
Upgrading yourself and never being slow!

You have created a legacy with your story
You have created history with your glory!

Dedication, persistence, and
beliefs are the rules
One creates history using
these tools!

Creating history
was only resultant
What you become
in the process
is most important!

You crossed over your
own limitations
You made the most
of all situations!

Creating the history was
secondary
Becoming the highest
version of yourself and
who you became in
the process was more
important and primary!

When we are connected
to our Super-Being,
all is possible!

When one decides to alter his life, one embarks on the journey of self-discovery and living the life with the fullest expression. One creates history for oneself and for generations to come. The poem describes the journey of such a person. It also informs about the tools through which it is done. More than the accomplishment of goals, it is the process which is important, remarkable, and beautiful. One becomes the highest version of oneself in this pursuit.

GLOSSARY

Line:

4 unravelled: solve or undo something complicated or puzzling.

6 revelling: getting great pleasure from a situation or an experience.

8 fabric without a crease: life without pressure, crushing.

10 sedative: suggestive of needing external support to remain calm and happy.

14 ploy: a plan with intention to turn the situation to our own advantage.

15 fray: with reference to internal fight, struggle to uplift oneself.

18 paying this fee: implies paying the price in the form of constantly working to imbibe higher values within oneself. Among this effort, constantly working to develop an attitude of giving and serving is the key to achieving success.

19 your time in a row: consecutive success; accomplishing all objectives one by one.

23 legacy: passing of name, fame, and property from one generation to the next. Creating something remarkable for future generations.

32 highest version of yourself: leading life with the best expression of oneself, getting back to one's quintessential self; living life with fullest potential.

23. Universe Beside on A Beautiful Long Ride

In a chauffeur-driven car we both sat side by side
Universe usually bumps in when one decides and plans to go for a beautiful long ride!

Lovingly, I offered him my adjacent seat
It was graceful he accepted this treat!

Slowly the conversation starts on a friendly note
The usual way seemed more elegant than I can quote

Lined up with trees
And decked up with nature's incredible show!

Universe kept listening to all, what I had to say
It has its own way, to communicate, teach, and pay!

It paused and smiled at each struggle
The bumpy road seemed now less troubled!

He was giving me his undivided attention
The pathways were forgotten as the valleys we entered!

Soon we were floating in air
I looked at the Universe with a lovingly stare!

To my surprise he kept on listening
The stories seemed never ending!

Not even once he asked
A long distance had already passed!

The destination nowhere in sight
I was curious to listen to my friend's advice!

Realising the situation, he lovingly spoke
To my surprise he spilled out a joke!

He said "all shows are created by me on the way"
Sometimes they're bumpy, sometimes they toss and sway!

Sometimes to help you enjoy the lined-up trees
Sometimes to make you feel at peace with the cooling breeze!

The way sometimes leading to valley
Sometimes to laughter arising from the belly!

I was amazed at this revelation
The ride now seemed more like a celebration!

This was the worthiest of rides
Having Universe as the friend beside!

The destination now seemed very near, the path very clear
We continued amusing each other very dear!

I would not leave him unless we arrived
Nor would he leave me on this beautiful and bumpy ride!

Lo! I can see the final destination
We arrived with much delight and jubilation!

The world was waiting to welcome this ride
All roads are shorter and beautiful with the Universe beside!

Universe is now ready for another ride
To make sure more and more travellers arrive at their
destination sitting beside!

Life seems to have many challenges. many internal and external ups and down. When one with faith decides to alter his life, the Universal help steps in and guides from all directions. It is like the Universe travelling with us in our journey. The above poem is one such journey wherein the Universe guides one while sitting beside. The journey becomes most beautiful in spite of the challenges at both internal and external levels. One arrives at the destination with delight and jubilation. Life's journey becomes a celebration. The Universal guidance is infinite and abundant and is open to all, it is apparently present to everyone who is prepared and willing to ask and accept and move along with determination and faith.

GLOSSARY

Line:

1 chauffeur: employed to drive a vehicle; suggesting luxury, universal abundance.

2 bumps in: to meet someone unexpectedly.

2 decides and plans: decision; plans include the desire and intention for achieving something with a clear direction of actions to be taken. Universal help arrives when one clearly decides and plans to alter his life.

6 usual way: usual life, routine life.

8 decked up: put on special attire to appear particularly appealing and attractive.

13 undivided attention: with full concentration.

16 lovingly stare: look upon adoringly with love.

25 all shows are created by me on the way: ups and down of life.

26 sway: move from side by side.

43 another ride: to help another seeker,

44 sitting beside: accompanying, refers to universal support, guidance one receives while working through the infinite source.

24. Say Yes to Dreams

Say yes to your dreams
Lay a continuous joyful stream!

Dreams make people what they ought to be
They lay the foundation for an excited present and future leap!

With dreams one can make most beautiful castles out of thin air
To abundance and riches infinite one can dare!

It was long ago that the Wright brothers dreamt to fly like birds
Whereas someone dreamt to change thoughts into words!

Someone to travel into outer space
And someone dreamt to win the Olympic race!

Someone dreamt to break a world record
Someone dreamt to change travel like Henry ford!

Dreams made Gandhi achieve the freedom
Whereas the comic Chaplin made new records breaking boredom!

It inspired someone to create lifesaving vaccine
Someone to write phenomenal books like Ruskin!

It gave the motive to wirelessly connect the world
It transformed the world into an e-world!

Continents and countries are brought so close
We are so much nearer than ever before!

Dreams have shaped our inner and outer space
It has changed our patterns, thoughts, taste, and race!

A child dreams and makes his way
Getting older, why are one's dreams
taken away?

To dream is everyone's right
It can change oneself and the world at sight!

To dream is the ordeal divine
It has turned sour grapes into sweet wine!

Saying yes to our dreams lays the foundation
To the divine Universal laws intervention!

It sets the pattern in place
To achieve anything in space!

Dream sets the energy in motion
It can unearth gold and magical potion!

The one who dreams raises the bar
It has turned simple carts into powerful cars!

Fill your dreams with passion and love
Feel them, be them, and give them an imaginative perk!

Say yes to your dreams, believe them and trust
Your belief and faith will raise them to the surface from the depths of the deepest crust!

Dreams are what make a person be. They characterize our purpose and objectives in life. Phenomenal successes have been attained by those who dreamt for possibilities and pursued them with passion, earnestness, and faith in achieving them. It has led to countless inventions and discoveries from ancient times. Things and situations which appeared impossible have been achieved. The process keeps on going and is an integral part of the incredible human journey. Dreams, as it were, give magical wings to human thoughts and actions by which they fly and go beyond the horizon. They bring to the surface appearances hiding in deep recesses and in the innermost core.

GLOSSARY

Line:

1 say yes: accept with conviction; agree.

4 future leap: being proactive and not waiting for life to happen to you; taking charge of the future.

5 castles out of thin air: plans seemingly very difficult to reach, nearly impossible tasks.

8 thoughts into words: putting down feelings in words; to write.

18 e-world: electronic world we are living in; information technology has almost connected everything via the Internet.

22 race: physical, behavioural, and cultural attributes; refers to human race, ethnicity.

26 at sight: as soon as someone or something has been seen.

27 ordeal: an experience.

34 magical potion: magical drink, elixir; believed that the one who drinks will live forever, or stay young.

35 raises the bar: raise standards or expectations.

38 imaginative perk: make advantageous; give extra with imagination.

40 deepest crust: refers to both external and internal recess, lying deep down.

I am always with you.
Be brave, have courage
and love life.

25. Universe Wishes to Co-Create

Universe wishes to co-create
Are you ready for this date?

It wishes to express through us
It is the only motive, please trust!

It wishes to lay down its divine presence
Through us it wishes to break all limitations!

Universe is the power sublime
It needs the being to go divine!

It wants to see them expressing fully
Leaving aside all their folly!

Co-creation is a celestial dance
Universe wishing to unveil its multiple stance!

Why not we allow it to co-create?
The reality and results we ourselves will be amazed!

Universe is the electricity
It needs the bulb to express its luminosity!

We are the bulb, it is the source
Both needed to perform, and perforce!

Universal abundance is everywhere
To this fact it makes us aware!

That abundance is our birth right
Why to scarcity then we subscribe?

It is ready to unfold
The stories to us untold!

The only exchange is faith and love
To believe gratefully that we can serve!

It is ready to embrace
Celebrating with us and to us emplace!

Universe is seemingly the spiritual, and we the physical entity
Both partnering in this subtle reality!

It's time to understand this simple process
Pull the straps, pass the test, and with inexhaustible joy, relax!

If we assume the Universe as our partner, it becomes ready for the co-creation, working together. Life then becomes a collaborative journey with the Universe. With Infinite Source working with us, there is nothing one can't achieve or accomplish. Let alone the peace and joy which flows from such joint venture.

The only requisites are faith, love, and the feeling of gratefulness and being ready to serve.

The higher power becomes the spiritual, and we the physical expression in the time, space, and reality working and co creating together. The process is simple and one can tune into this easily. One will be amazed by the reality and results arising from this alignment.

GLOSSARY

Line:

1 co create: create jointly; working together.

7 sublime: of extreme excellence or beauty.

11 celestial dance: divine dance, heavenly show; appearing in Hindu and Buddhist mythology.

16 luminosity: brilliance or radiance; having intrinsic brightness or light.

18 perforce: essential, necessary, or inevitable.

28 emplace: to put in place or position.

30 subtle reality: difficult to perceive or understand; elusive, not seemingly obvious.

32 inexhaustible: incapable of depletion; abundant.

26. Include Your Story

The world is waiting for your glory
It is your time to shine and include your story!

The stories amuse and thrill the reader
It's time to become your own leader!

We have infinite potential in store
Why not express when the world is asking for more?

Skipping levels and taking a quantum leap
Sowing the seeds which one can reap!

The world needs your words to hear
It's long been playing with fear!

What is stopping you? Cut that chain!
From the dust massive storms have rained!

It is time to break your limiting beliefs
To cross oceans and unknown peaks!

The success stories are made of such heroic deeds
They arise from the strong needs!

One needs to ignite the passion
Lead the way with wisdom and compassion!

The world is waiting for your full expression
Do away with all inner suppression!

The story inside is taking shape
One more effort is needed to make!

Limiting beliefs, paradigms, and mindset
Will resist this approach
One by one undo their encroach!

Their power limited when one decides
To reach the height and reveal the might!

Follow what kindles your heart
It's now time to make a start!

Ages have gone by waiting for your show
Now shoot the arrows one by one in a row!

With persistent efforts, faith, and gratitude
One can attain any altitude!

It does not require great talents or complex allegory
It's your time to shine and arrive with your own story!

One often feels that success and fame arrives to people with extraordinary talents or through inheritance. But in fact, each of us can be the cradle of success if we believe in ourselves and are ready to unfold our story to the world.

Persistent efforts, faith, and gratitude are keys for this path-breaking journey. The world is full of numerous such success stories of individuals who have taken the world by storm. They have achieved phenomenal success at all levels—not only for themselves, but also for the people around them. Hence, the first step is the feeling of worthiness and belief that one can alter his life and bring his story to the world.

Success is not a prerogative only in the hands of a few or a particular class of people. It is open for one and all, just as Universal abundance is open to one and all. With a strong belief system in place, the right mindset, and working upon and altering one's limiting beliefs and paradigms, one is surely on the path of success within a very short span of time.

GLOSSARY

Line:

7 skipping levels: jumping and arriving to higher levels.

7 quantum leaps: a huge, often sudden, increase or advancement.

10 playing with fears: living with fears; fears become overpowering.

12 rained: to fall, arrived.

15 heroic deeds: courageous acts.

23 limiting beliefs: beliefs holding one back; putting constraints and limitation on abilities and true potential, leading to the impoverishing of life.

23 paradigms: habitual way of perceiving, doing, acting, or living.

25 encroach: to gradually take control of someone's rights, property, responsibility; intrude. Refers to encroachment by limiting the beliefs or paradigms on one's life.

31 shoot the arrows one by one in row: the arrows signify direction, force, movement, power and direction of travel, whereas "one by one in a row" signifies a continuous succession. One after another. Refers to consistent and persistent efforts with earnestness in a particular direction and with continuous succession.

34 allegory: use of story, picture, or a narrative to deliver a broader message.

27. Invest in Yourself

One fact I learnt hard and deep
That to invest in oneself is the most essential everyday need!

One's whole life one usually invests
To things other than oneself it mostly rests!

Even the wisest investor misses this insider call
That investment in oneself is the most beneficial of all!

All our time, energy, efforts, and money are invested
To add value to one's own inner being is generally neglected!

One buys the land, the gold, and the shares
To upgrade oneself one hardly cares!

To trivial and petty things, one keeps subscribing
The Infinite Source within us is left always wanting!

To the latest gadgets we quickly and eagerly upgrade
Seldom our mindset and beliefs are surveyed, altered, and weighed!

Adding external assets is prudent, well, and good
But to add internal assets also demands a serious thought which one should!

This is the best service to oneself one can render
One who fails to do so, bids the highest tender!

Through gratitude, discipline, faith, and consistency we move up in this holy trip
We keep learning new skills and adding to our portfolio the scrips blue chip!

By upgrading our self with regular study and applying wisdom
We learn to optimise our internal kingdom!

When we are open to the Universal laws
We are saved from sharp downfall and penetrating claws!

One who remains stuck to the obsolete system
Fails to upgrade and change the internal algorithm and terms!

One who keeps adding and installing new beliefs and learnings
Succeeds in decoding the pattern which helps in substantial earnings!

One changes his life and aspires to be better
To the new joys he lay open his platter!

Let us welcome the fun and joy and aspire for long term gains
Do away with trivial yearnings and pains!

Investing in oneself I found most productive
Realised deeply that Universal abundance is not selective!

It is open to one and all
One needs to invest wisely to minimise the impact and be immune to each great rise and fall!

The inner assets give enormous returns
Dividend and bonuses each day we earn!

Peace, prosperity, joy, and happiness
Are the way of growth of this most notable and worthy investment!

It works on the same principle of external investing
The returns are fabulous and compounding!

The way is very similar to systematic investment planning
Investment in oneself makes our daily lives extremely charming!

Step by step we learn the skill
The most fertile-barren land we successfully till!

When we invest and learn to tap our own infinite potential
and greatness
We pave the way through this sound investment and
embrace uniqueness!

The knowledge acts like the antivirus
It prevents one from a sudden crash and enables to de-stress!

Making now, this firm resolve
By investing, upgrading, and updating our inner system we
sooner evolve!

Investment in one's own self must be taken on priority and by all means. One who continues investing in oneself and upgrading his skills both internally and externally is the prudent investor in the longer run. Often, we neglect the very need to invest in our own inner being by putting in time, energy, efforts, and even money. One continues to neglect the inner for the outer and pays the price.

The poem welcomes the investment in various asset classes, but at the same time puts great emphasis on investment on the inner asset class, which one usually misses out on. The investment in inner assets works on the same principle of external investing. Through step-by-step systematic investment planning on inner assets, one arrives to his desired goals and receives handsome overall returns. It is suggestive that investing in oneself is the wisest investment one can make not only for oneself but for their family as well. One reaps its abundant benefits for a long, long time.

GLOSSARY

Line:

1 hard and deep: learnt through setbacks and internal assessment and deeper thought process to overcome them.

5 insider call: information coming from a person who has some special advantage or influence while advising for investing in stock market; in reference to the poem it refers to one's self for the information coming from within (inner calling).

14 surveyed, altered, and weighed: make changes after careful examination and assessment of a situation.

18 bids the highest tender: pays the highest price

20 blue chip scrips: a blue chip is a well-recognized, well-established, and financially sound company. Blue chip companies are known to weather downturns and operate profitably in the face of adverse economic conditions, which helps to contribute to their long record of stable and reliable growth.

24 penetrating: able to make a way through or into something; refers to situations having deep impact.

26 algorithm: process or set of rules to be followed in calculations or other problem-solving operations.

28 decoding the pattern: analysing or interpreting a repeated way of thought and action and converting it into a different way of thought and action for achieving higher and better results

32 trivial yearnings: intense longing for insignificant things; of very little importance or value.

36 great rise and fall: pairs of opposites; suggesting very favourable and unfavourable situations in the marketplace or in life.

43 systematic investment planning: a periodic and a regular contribution to the investment with a definite end in mind.

46 fertile-barren land: pairs of opposites; suggesting land though fertile remains barren. Our minds are most fertile land, and whatever thoughts we plant we will get similar results in life. It requires earnest efforts to plant the right and positive thoughts and thereby achieving fruitful results.

46 till: prepare the land for crops to be planted by ploughing and fertilizing; cultivate.

28. The Creative Process (Divine Process)

The reader would be utterly curious and confused
To know how to put the creative process in use?!

It is the key to all success
As opposed to the competitive process!

It is the foundation of every goal
One has to understand and play a deep role!

One has to set the momentum
To act in accordance with the creative substratum!

The creative process is simple to learn in an instance
One needs unwavering faith and ceaseless feeling of gratitude on the formless substance!

It is being in harmony with the infinite intelligence
Which is creative and never competitive in its due diligence!

It is working in cooperation and being imaginative
With the formless substance most cooperative and superlative!

One who remains established in this creative plane
The Universe sets a motion of abundance and fame!

Understanding the creative process is the key
It is to the Universe, the favourite divine plea!

Put all your imagination to the test
Unless you grab the concept, don't rest!

Achieve
Conceive

Conceiving, believing, becoming, and achieving are the four steps
One who understands never regrets!

One who conceives and projects the goal with faith, gratitude, and with his whole heart and soul
Understanding well the concept and playing in advance the winner's role!

To him the Universe lovingly unfolds
Its secrets and beauty ever untold!

The one grasping it rightly
Is now in harmony and in alignment with Almighty!

The process is clear and simple
We need to "be" to create the ripple!
The Universe is always ready to give
Just "believe and become" what one conceives to achieve!

Between the conceive and achieve are two miraculous blanks
One who can fill in these blanks with 'believe' and 'become' can bridge the two banks 'conceive' and 'achieve' with the planks and achieves the desired rank.

It is the reverse of the conventional "A, B, C, D" alphabet order and system
Where "D, C, B, A" is in the opposite sequence in the creative process decode and term
Where "D" stands for Divine (Creative) process, "C" for conceive, "B" for believe and become, and "A" for achieve
These alphabets "as if" in the reverse order being laid down by the super accorder and the most generous rewarder!

The ancient wisdom teaches this simple mantra
Why consume our time, efforts, and energy in various tantra?

This is the elixir the ancient Sermon preach
One who believeth, one becomes and finally reach!

The quantum physics reveals the same fact
One attains the reality to what it "believes and becomes" the vibrational match!

Feelings and deep gratitude are most important, essential, and vital
To letting the creative process make a grand arrival!

Let the Universe know your clear intentions
Then "believe and become" the person!

Leave the rest to the nature's call
And let the magic and miracles one by one roll!

Life is a constant celebration
The Universe is ready to participate and is welcoming us onboard in this co-creation!

To the one who works in perfect alignment and harmonious resonance
With the most generous and kind, the formless substance!

Creative (Divine) Process mathematical equation and explanation:

Achieve = Conceive + Believe + Become

A = C + B + B

Hence:

A = C + 2B

Conceive ______________________________

Believe ______________________________ Achieve

Become ______________________________

The formless substance is ever giving. It is abundant in its disposition. It is "as it were" trying to live and enjoy through humanity. It seeks the expression through us. It wants us to cultivate our talents to the fullest and provide us with the means in all ways. The desire of the formless substance for a fuller and better living has caused and will continue to cause all the abundance available in nature. When one realises it and gives his clear intention to the formless substance, all the divine forces are set in motion.

Hence, making your intentions clear to the Universe is the first step. We also commonly refer to this as projecting the goals and purpose. Then comes the process of believing and becoming the one that is being desired and finally achieving it. This is the functioning of the creative process or the divine process.

But usually, we are so accustomed to seeing, hearing, touching, smelling, and tasting (by our senses) before believing and becoming, and hence creeps in the doubt on the functionality of the creative process. Clear purpose and intention—coupled with faith and gratitude—are the key for believing and becoming, and finally achieving.

In the entire process earnest efforts and actions are continuously needed to finally achieve or receive what is desired. It is to say, "by the right thoughts the things are brought to us, and by the right actions we receive them." One who can put into practice the right methods and follow the Creative process, achieves whatever is conceived within the due course of time.

GLOSSARY

Line:

1 curious and confused: eager to know with a feeling of being puzzled or bewildered at once.

4 competitive process: In this process the underlying belief is that resources are limited, and one has to compete to achieve or else they will be left behind. This is operating in a competitive process with a scarcity mindset as opposed to the creative process which believes there is abundance all around. In the Universe, supplies are inexhaustible, and resources are infinite.

8 creative substratum: foundation or basis of a creative process.

11 infinite intelligence: Universal energy, supreme consciousness; Brahman as termed in the Vedanta and Upanishads (ancient Indian scriptures).

14 superlative: of the highest quality or degree.

18 divine plea: a request made to be addressed on a priority coupled with emotions and feelings; made to the divine power, Universe.

30 create the ripple: create a wave-like motion; implying a momentum which gradually leads to several other events one after the other.

38 super accorder and the most generous rewarder: divine power, the Universe, formless substance, the Almighty.

44 vibrational match: believing and becoming what one desires to achieve; experiencing the feeling that it is already done or achieved.

47 your clear intentions: specific desires or goals.

53 perfect alignment: the proper adjustment of components for a coordinated functioning, working in sync. To be in alignment with oneself implies all aspects of ourselves working in perfect harmony and operating to serve our highest good.

53 harmonious resonance: moving in unison, free from disagreement or dissent.

54 formless substance: Universal energy, supreme consciousness. Brahman as termed in the Vedanta and Upanishads (very ancient and timeless Indian scriptures).

SURF

29. Come Friends, Let's Go to the Beach

Today for our own glorious journey we reach
Come friends, let's go to the beach!

The poems narrated in the book are not to preach and win
They are my stories and narratives from deep search within
Through them to the world I have attempted to reach
Come friends, let's go to the beach!

The sea is waiting for long
The sands today have taken the vow strong
They all wish to touch our feet
Come friends, let's go to the beach!

Palms swaying in joy for our arrival
Pelicans and albatross over the seas searching for food for survival
Conches and seashells are laid around
Children playing in sand and merry go around
Let's take a pause from routine and breach
Come friends, let's go to the beach!

Let's make sandcastles with wider lanes
Wash in oceans are deep down stains
Let's relax and experience this beauty
To our souls we also have some duty
The great oceans convey this lesson and teach
Come friends, let's go to the beach!

The sky is ever changing in a colourful show
The birds flying over in a row
The sound of the sea is loud and soothing
Timeless sand grains have their own stories to preach
Come friends, let's go to the beach!

Put on your shoes, bring on your song
For one can never go wrong
Give yourself a new uplift
The horizon in sight is trying to outreach
Come friends, let's go to the beach!

Far away some birds are chirping
To the sound of the waves they are unknowingly matching
Together they are both music to ears
This opportunity has arrived after many years
Wake up to this glory and reach
Come friends, let's go to the beach!

We are just like the ocean and seas
Vast and infinite in definition and ease
Going to the beach is touching that chord
It's meeting our own self and consort
The seas are waiting for so long for us to reach
Come friends, let's go to the beach!

Going to the beach is a symbolic poem whereby one invites others to come to the threshold of their knowledge and wisdom and see the panoramic beauty which the seas offer to the human senses. A true teacher inviting earnest seekers to the beach as he knows they are vast and magnanimous like the great ocean and seas, the journey of the human soul is timeless and eternal. Their arrival symbolises achieving their own highest potential and living life with the fullest version of themselves.

GLOSSARY

Line:

12 Pelicans and albatross over the seas searching for food for survival: people endlessly searching for sustenance; struggling for survival, existence.

13 Conches and seashells are laid around: the human mind misses the jewels of self-knowledge and his fullest expression; merely struggling for existence.

24 The birds flying over in a row: denotes earnest seekers working steadily to uplifting themselves.

25 The sound of the sea is loud and soothing: suggesting life is full of pair of opposites.

26 Timeless sand grains: the formation of the beach and its origin is unknown, very similar to the human soul which is timeless and eternal.

28 bring on your song: bring on your purpose, aim.

29 For one can never go wrong: a person with a definite purpose in life can never go wrong. He knows for sure about its accomplishment.

34 To the sound of the waves they are unknowingly matching: nature having a unique way to function in an orchestra.

42 consort: companion.

30. Welcoming the Paradigm Shift

Let us welcome the paradigm shift.
Life is waiting for us; let's do away with all drift and internal rift!

The pandemic has been a blessing in disguise.
Let us to greater achievements organise!

Rightly thinking into our way for riches
Creating our own niches!

The Universe is ready to co-create
Let us take positive steps to be free and liberate!

Tapping and learning new ways
Creating each day an amazing day!

Let the negative energies go in vain
Filling the void with zest and erasing all stains and pains!

Let us do away with our limiting beliefs,
Life is ready for joy and treat!

Converting the wishes to conceiving, believing, and becoming is the key to go
The progress may be slow but one hundred percent sure!

Transforming our desires to definite goals
Life is ready to give us infinite roles.

That's the way our mentors and teachers preach,
Nothing is beyond our reach!

old paradigms limiting beliefs
and gratitude
Thank you

With action, steadfast faith, and inspiration
We can accomplish any destination!

Life is ready to embrace,
Only the right thoughts can bring solace!

Steering our ways with affirmations and visualisation,
Marching and celebrating we create our new situation!

We walk with a magic wand of thanks and gratitude in hand
Life is offering new altitudes on stands!

The Universe is ready with its celestial show
Abundance is the way to go!

We are entering the new realm and welcoming this relief
From our old paradigms and limiting beliefs!

Rejoice while they break, and celebrate while they go
They were the ones which held us from our glorious show!

Release them to the winds and put an end to all rift
Cheerfully we welcome this new Paradigm shift.

The poem welcomes the new shift by changing old behavioural patterns and paradigms. An earnest learner works step by step towards changing his habitual ways of doing things and replaces them with new thoughts and actions, thereby changing the result. One's own limiting beliefs, paradigms bind oneself. Though they seem hard to break, but with earnest effort they can be replaced and replenished with new beliefs and patterns. Life is abundant and peaceful with this new positive shift. It also explains the process through which it can be achieved in a simple way.

GLOSSARY

Line:

1 paradigm: habitual way of perceiving, doing, acting, or living. Paradigms are the programming and conditioning of the subconscious mind that controls the behaviour and produces the result; they are as how one lives his life. Paradigm shift implies changing the behaviour, habitual patterns, reprogramming or reconditioning the subconscious mind and thereby finally changing the results in life. Changing of the cause; behavioural pattern to change the result.

2 drift: slow movement, carried away, blown away.

2 rift: break, split, a crack.

6 own niches: a place or position suitable or appropriate for a person or thing.

7 Universe is ready to co-create: work together; work hand in hand. Physically express through you.

9 tapping: quick light blow, striking.

12 erasing all stains and pains: erasing unhappy events from the past.

12 filling the void: to provide or replace; replenish something that's needed.

15 converting the wishes to conceiving, believing, and becoming: the process by which a desire is converted to the feeling of owning, believing, and becoming. The feeling with conviction that the end is achieved already. The creative process.

24 bring solace: bring peace; comfort.

28 new altitudes on stands: making available; offering new heights.

29 celestial show: relating to divinity, heavenly bliss, supremely good.

34 glorious show: our highest expression; living life to the fullest potential; being the best version of oneself.

*When we are connected
to our Super-Being,
all is possible!*

ABOUT THE AUTHOR

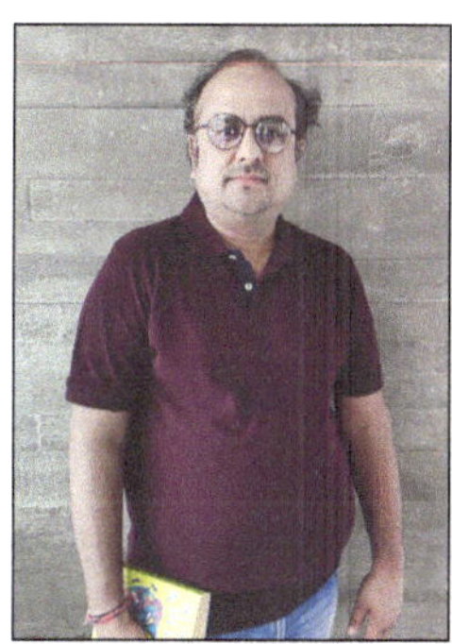

Sandeep Mangeram Agarwal is a partner in a successful business firm dealing in imported textile yarns and manufacturing fabrics. After beginning his career while still undergoing his university education, he has now accumulated nearly twenty-five years of professional experience in textiles.

Sandeep was born in the small town of Hisar, nearly 167 kilometres to the north from the capital of India, New Delhi. He currently resides in the city of Surat in western India, situated on the Arabian sea, famous for textiles and diamonds.

He lives with his wife and their fourteen-year-old son.

MY LIFE AND JOURNEY

I have seven sisters, and I am the only son to my parents. In India during those years, having a male child was believed to be almost essential in keeping the family legacy and lineage. So, every time a child was expected my parents would eagerly await my arrival. These days, things have totally changed, and most couples have only one or two children—many a times only a daughter. My mother use to tell me stories of how she awaited my birth so eagerly that she would visit all the temples and seek the blessings of sages and saints and would incessantly offer prayers each day and night to have a boy being born into our family. Finally, around midnight on the 14th of February 1975, I came into the world. My birth brought much joy to my family, especially to my parents. In the dark nightly hours, my birth was like the most beautiful dawn for them, as they so eagerly awaited my arrival with all their heart and soul—a very long wait for them indeed. My birth fulfilled their very mission and purpose in life. I was the eighth child.

The seventh daughter in our family, born before me, was brought up as a boy, and I feel now and can connect that somehow my parent's visualizing and believing in her as a boy, dressing her as boy, and giving her all the attributes of the boy helped them to finally create the reality which they wanted to see in form of me: a boy being born to them and a brother to the seven sisters. Learning how to create reality through the creative process is shared in the poem "The Creative Process (Divine Process)." How conceiving, believing, and becoming is the key to finally achieving is explained in the poem. In all our childhood family albums, she (my sister) can be always be seen wearing boyish attire in all the photographs as usual.

The connection with the Universe, as I can now relate to my own son who is the same age as I was when the spiritual father, the Universe, held my hand during my journey. Just as I am helping my son in his journey, similarly, the Universe has helped me in crossing over all my internal and external hurdles as they have arrived. I can so vividly see its help always in all my endeavours. It has helped me to break my paradigms and limiting beliefs, and is giving me the love, help, and all the attention I need from it as a son

An ordinary and simple journey made incredible, most extraordinary, and beautiful with faith and gratitude by the love and blessings of 'The Infinite Source'- The Universal providence and the provider of all joy, happiness, abundance, and guidance to each one of us and to all!

WHY THIS BOOK?

After losing my father at the age of twelve and then my mother when I was twenty-eight, I have been guided, as it were, by the Universal father and mother, the Infinite Source. I am making my way through all the ups and downs, crossing the journey with faith and gratitude.

Covid-19 and the long lockdowns that followed changed our perspective of the world and our relationship with it. It gave us the opportunity to deeply assess within ourselves and render ourselves to arrive at a conclusion of many new thoughts lying dormant which were brought to the surface through this deep internal assessment.

Old paradigms and limiting beliefs were set aside and a new journey of self-discovery was on its way. It was as if waking up from a deep slumber, guided by the divine light all around, illuminating the way and path.

Working Through the Infinite Source is one such journey of a young boy making his way out and sharing what he has acquired throughout his life. A journey of almost thirty years compiled by way of thirty poems; guided most lovingly by the Infinite Source, as a loving father and mother guiding their sons and daughters on their journey!

The deepest urge was to share my learnings acquired and learnt over the years so that they may help and add value to the readers in their journey as well. I can proudly say that it has been an incredible journey of faith and gratitude.

With joy in my heart and with love and deep gratitude to all the galaxy of people, guides, mentors, teachers, family members, and friends—and foremost to my parents and my spiritual father and mother, the Universe—this work is presented by the Infinite Source through me. I am only the channel by which the Infinite Source shares this entire journey.

The poem “Universe is My Father” is about the journey of a father and son wherein the Universe is the father, and I am the son. The poem “Lighthouse” is the reflection of my deep feelings, and thereafter an internal assessment during the long lockdowns followed by Covid-19 and the help and guidance I received in form of lighthouses (various people throughout the world).Wherein the poem “Universe Wishes to Co-Create” is about how the Universal creative energy in the form of mother guiding us to co create our reality and helping us to be the highest expression of ourself.

I am deeply grateful for all the help and guidance I have received throughout my life and will continue to receive in abundance at all times by the divine grace.

From a time early in my life, I have felt as if the divine guidance, the Universe, holding my hand and helping me tread this beautiful journey we call life with magic, awe, and miracles at each turn. Each poem in the book is a reflection of those lessons learned and the divine grace I most lovingly received by Working through the Infinite Source.

Namaste!

Thank you!

Sandeep

For more information about the author, please visit:

http://sandeepmagarwal.com/

Sandeep Agarwal

Sandeep.M.Agarwal

https://www.linkedin.com/in/sandeep-agarwal-6a8a22203/

With every donation, a voice will be given to the creativity that lies within the hearts of our children living with diverse challenges.

By making this difference, children that may not have been given the opportunity to have their Heart Heard will have the freedom to create beautiful works of art and musical creations.

Donate by visiting

HeartstobeHeard.com

We thank you.

www.ingramcontent.com/pod-product-compliance
Lightning Source LLC
LaVergne TN
LVHW052251100826
845147LV00001B/17

* 9 7 8 1 9 8 9 7 5 6 8 5 0 *